CW0067311W

GET CHUGGING
HOW TO PLAY RHYTHM HARMONICA
BY BEN HEWLETT & PAUL LENNON

ONLINE AUDIO

To Access the Online Audio Go To:
www.melbay.com/20848BCDEB

Visit us on the Web at www.melbay.com — E-mail us at email@melbay.com

FOREWORD

The harmonica has largely been ignored as an instrument that can be easily taught in an organized way. Most people still think of it as a self-taught instrument used primarily for playing the blues. That is changing and Ben Hewlett has proved this in many schools and colleges in Southern England through his persistence and energy as he introduces his teaching methods in workshops and smaller group and individual lessons. Over 5,000 people have learned to chug with Ben! The play-along CD came from the need to have something musical and interesting to play along with at home as well as being easily accessible to anyone whether or not they had previous musical experience; particularly theoretical. This book contains the 'chugs' from every track on the album clearly notated as well as a transcription of the main melodies from those same tracks.

The overall course focuses on particular areas of harmonica playing from 'chugging' (rhythm playing) to single note playing, from note-bending to new repertoire with returns to the blues. It is all clearly explained and demonstrated and most of all is fun to do.

In my long association with Ben I have come to see that the diatonic (10-hole) harmonica is capable of a far greater range of styles and expression. In writing the music for the 'Chugging' CD I composed in a variety of styles and found that the harmonica suited all of them admirably.

I heartily recommend this course for beginners and more experienced players alike and hope that the potential of this 'humble' instrument can be more fully realized and expanded far beyond just the blues idiom.

Paul Lennon L.T.C.L. Beckenham, Kent UK Feb 2000

Ben Hewlett

Paul Lennon

'CHUGGING' Introduction

Welcome to part one of the Ben Hewlett Harmonica course. The first technique we will learn is called 'chugging' – playing the harmonica in a rhythmic fashion using chords, that's two or more notes at once and using words to create the rhythms. The idea is to use this book with your CD to see how the 'chugging' that you are already familiar with looks on paper. This book is designed to be used along with the CD to help you read music and see how it comes alive with the recordings.

Here's how it works:

First learn how to play all the 'chugging' phrases which only use holes 1, 2 & 3 on your 'C' diatonic harmonica. All instructions are on the CD, so put it on and start playing. These are found in part one of the book as well as at the beginning of each of the tunes.

As a supplement you can make up your own 'chugging' phrases to suit the music. It is probably best to turn the balance button to the left to lose the recorded harmonica sound.

Furthermore, when you can play single notes you are ready to go on to the tunes in part two. These are arranged as they appear on the CD and the suggested order of learning these pieces is 11, 1, 2, 3, 4, 5, 6, 8, 9, 7, and then 10.

Three of the tunes have duet sections: 2, 9 & 11. These can be played by two harmonicas or even with another treble clef instrument like violin or recorder.

Tablature or 'tab'. This is the system of numbers and arrows that tells the harmonica player which holes to use and whether to blow or draw. This also includes symbols that show when to bend notes; we teach bending in a later book.

You will find that the first tune has 'tab' on every note and then in the following tunes only when 'new' notes appear are they also 'tabbed'! This gives the harmonica player the chance to pencil in the tab for him or herself where necessary and then to rub it out when they're more familiar with the notes. A full chart is on page 45.

This book is dedicated to a great friend of ours and of the harmonica, Douglas Tate.

Douglas Tate (1934-2005)

USE THE CD FIRST

You can follow all the recorded instructions and go through the book later on.

This book is a supplement of written music to be used <u>after</u> you've been through all the CD tracks.

TABLE OF CONTENTS

PART 1

THE 'CHUGS'

Here's how the 'chugs' look when they're written down as musical notes.

Use holes 1, 2, and 3 for all tracks except CD track 35 (Woww).

1. Choo choo chooo (CD Track 3)

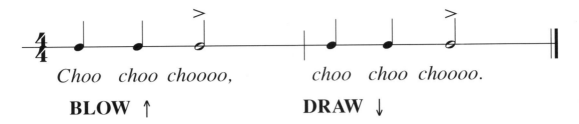

Choo   choo choooo,   choo   choo choooo.

BLOW ↑   **DRAW** ↓

2. Choo chacka choo (CD Track 5)

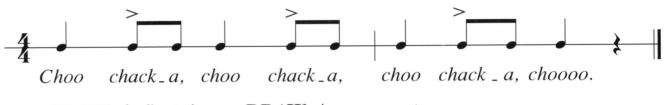

Choo   chack_a, choo   chack_a,   choo   chack_a, choooo.

BLOW ↑ **first time**   **DRAW** ↓ **on repeat**

3. Doo chicka (CD Track 7)

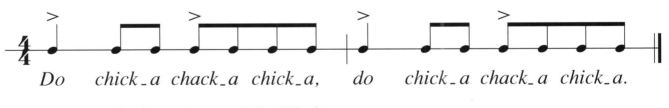

Do   chick_a chack_a chick_a,   do   chick_a chack_a chick_a.

BLOW ↑ **first time**   **DRAW** ↓ **on repeat**

4. Choo diddeley (CD Track 9)

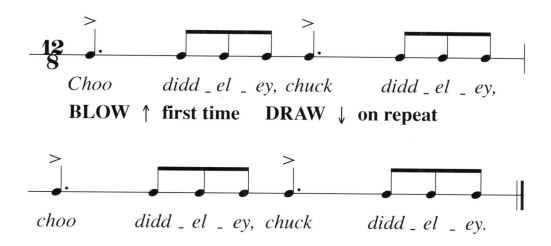

Choo   didd _ el _ ey, chuck   didd _ el _ ey,

BLOW ↑ **first time   DRAW** ↓ **on repeat**

choo   didd _ el _ ey, chuck   didd _ el _ ey.

5. Chow diddeley tock diddeley (CD Track 11)

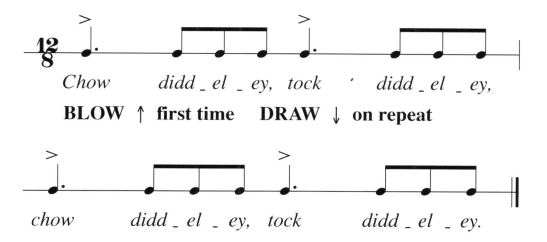

Chow   didd _ el _ ey, tock   didd _ el _ ey,

BLOW ↑ **first time   DRAW** ↓ **on repeat**

chow   didd _ el _ ey, tock   didd _ el _ ey.

6. Siggy saggy (CD Track 13)

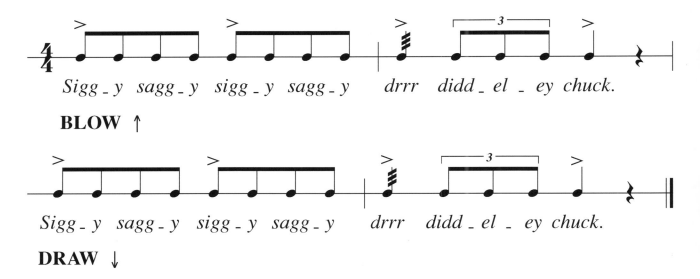

Note: Don't worry if you can't roll your 'RRR's especially breathing in; just make the sound of 'DRRR' like 'drag', 'drive', or 'drink' and all will be well.

7. Tooka chicka (CD Track 15)

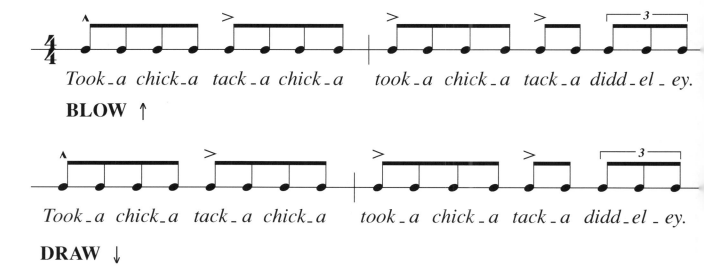

8. Zz acka (CD Track 17)

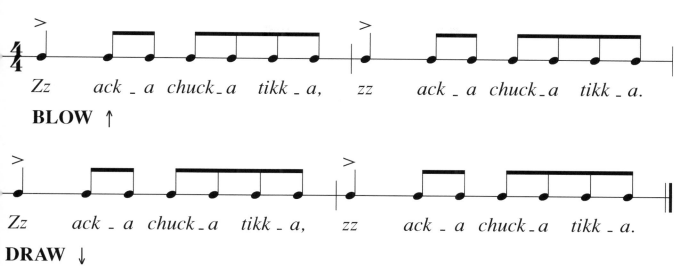

Zz   ack _ a chuck _ a tikk _ a,   zz   ack _ a chuck _ a tikk _ a.

BLOW ↑

Zz   ack _ a chuck _ a tikk _ a,   zz   ack _ a chuck _ a tikk _ a.

DRAW ↓

9. Drrr (CD Track 19)

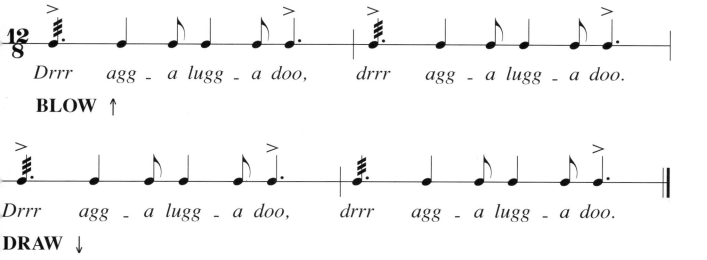

Drrr   agg _ a lugg _ a doo,   drrr   agg _ a lugg _ a doo.

BLOW ↑

Drrr   agg _ a lugg _ a doo,   drrr   agg _ a lugg _ a doo.

DRAW ↓

10. Chuckety tickety (CD Track 21)

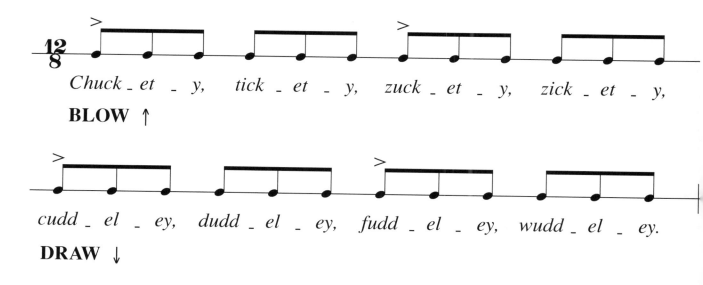

Chuck _ et _ y,   tick _ et _ y,   zuck _ et _ y,   zick _ et _ y,

BLOW ↑

cudd _ el _ ey,   dudd _ el _ ey,   fudd _ el _ ey,   wudd _ el _ ey.

DRAW ↓

11. I would like a chicken tikka (CD Track 23)

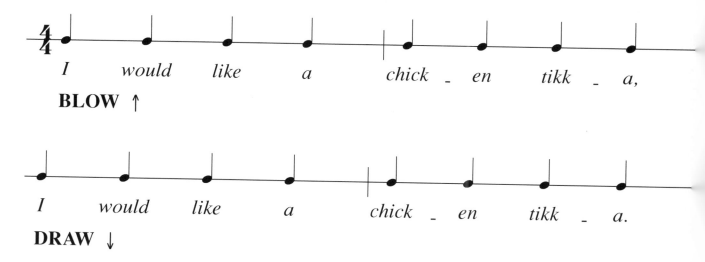

I   would   like   a   chick _ en   tikk _ a,

BLOW ↑

I   would   like   a   chick _ en   tikk _ a.

DRAW ↓

PART 2

THE TUNES

When you can play single notes you will be able to use these pages to play the tunes that accompany the chugs.

Where the 'tab' is missing you can find it on page 45 - pencil it into the music or better yet, learn to read the written music; it's not hard!

1. Choo (CD Track 3)

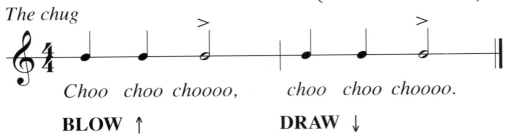

The chug

Choo choo choooo,   choo choo choooo.

BLOW ↑   **DRAW** ↓

The track

♩ = 162   *(Drums in)*

A 𝄋 (Chord symbols)

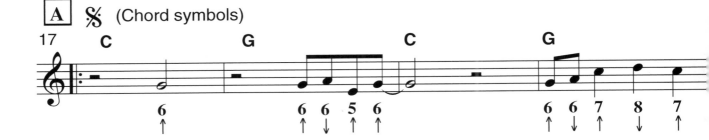

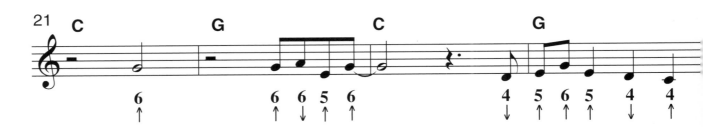

B | *Play tune 1st time only - improvise on chords 2nd time through*

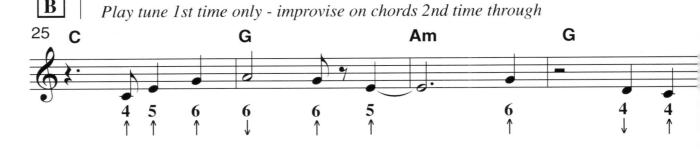

2. Choo Chaka (CD Track 5)

The chug

Choo chack_a, choo chack_a, choo chack_a, choooo.

BLOW ↑ **first time**   **DRAW** ↓ **on repeat**

The track ♩

C Solo Section

3. Doo chicka (CD Track 7)

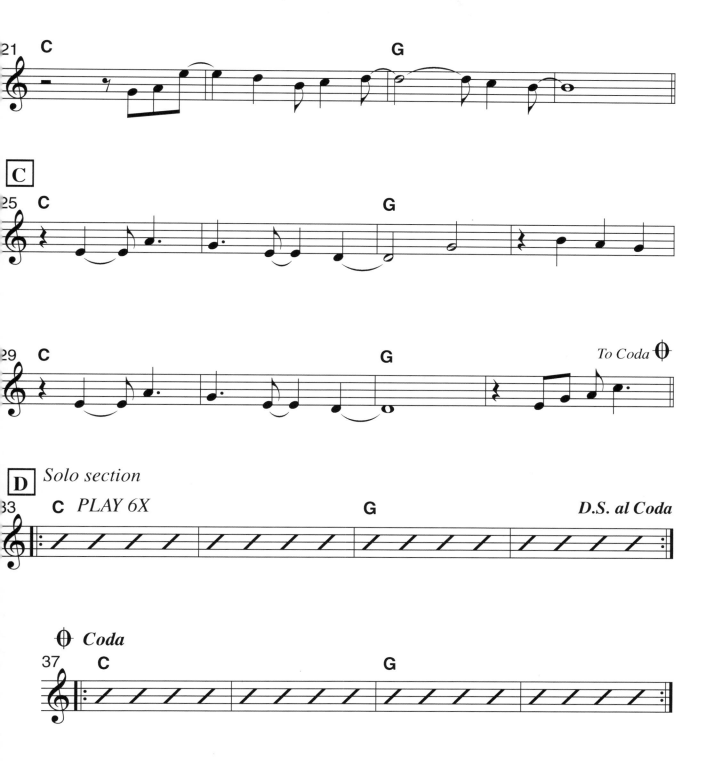

4. Choo diddley (CD Track 9)

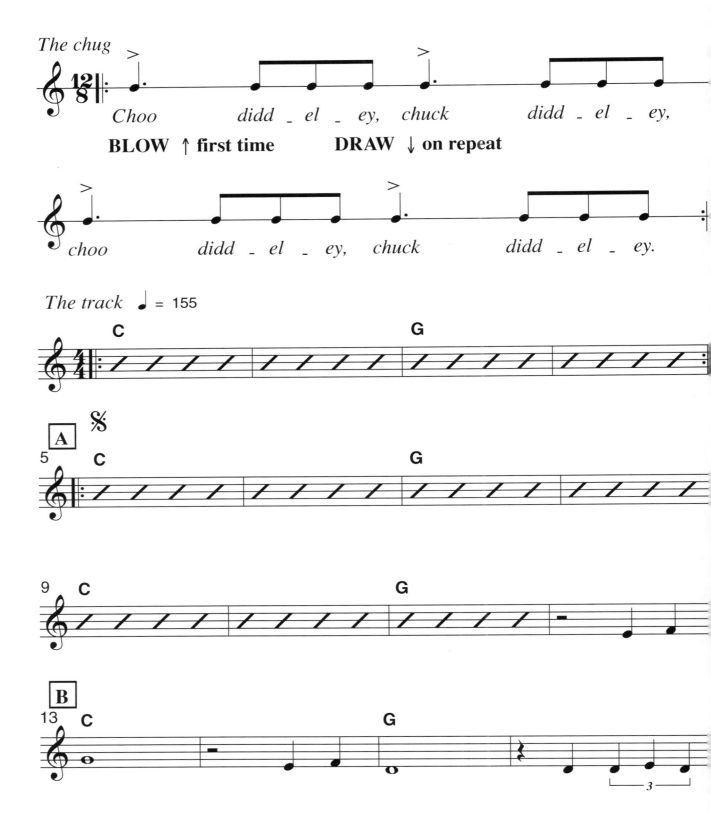

The chug

Choo didd _ el _ ey, chuck didd _ el _ ey,

BLOW ↑ first time   **DRAW ↓ on repeat**

choo didd _ el _ ey, chuck didd _ el _ ey.

The track ♩ = 155

C   G

A %

C   G

C   G

B

C   G

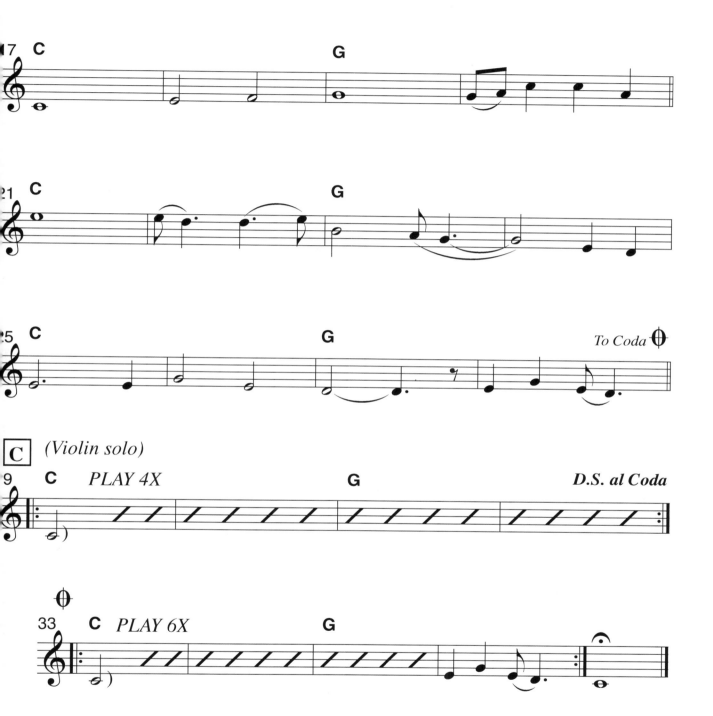

5. Chow diddeley (CD Track 11)

The chug

Chow   didd _ el _ ey,   tock   didd _ el _ ey,

BLOW ↑ first time   DRAW ↓ on repeat

chow   didd _ el _ ey,   tock   didd _ el _ ey.

The track ♩ = 154

C   G

A
5 C   *Guitar*   G

9 C   G

B
13 C   *Trumpet*   G

6. Siggy saggy (CD Track 13)

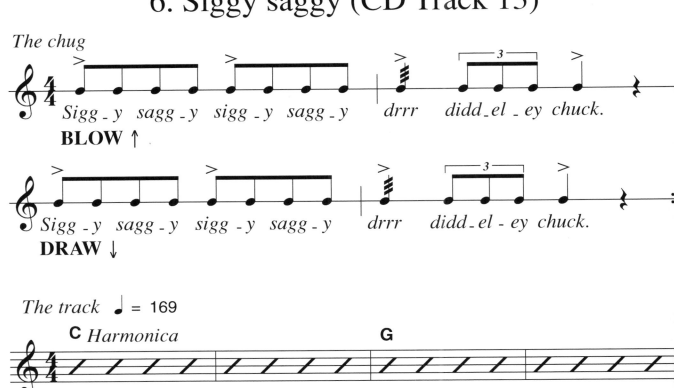

The chug

Sigg‿y sagg‿y sigg‿y sagg‿y drrr didd‿el‿ey chuck.

BLOW ↑

Sigg‿y sagg‿y sigg‿y sagg‿y drrr didd‿el‿ey chuck.

DRAW ↓

The track ♩ = 169

C *Harmonica*   **G**

Orch. drone
5 **C** *PLAY 4X*   **G**   **Fine**

Harmonica
9 **C** *PLAY 3X*   **G**

A *Guitar*
13 **C**   **G**

6. Siggy saggy (CD Track 13)

7. Tooka chika (CD Track 15)

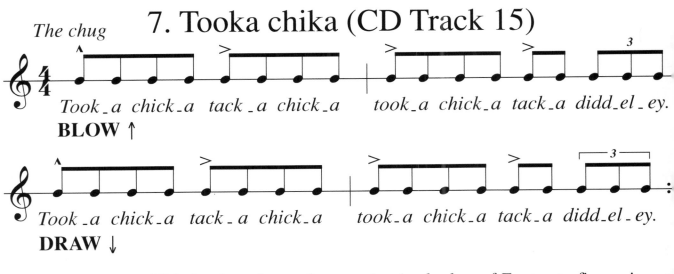

The chug

Took_a chick_a tack_a chick_a   took_a chick_a tack_a didd_el_ey.

BLOW ↑

Took_a chick_a tack_a chick_a   took_a chick_a tack_a didd_el_ey.

DRAW ↓

This is played on a harmonica in the key of F - try to figure it out.

The track ♩ = 95

C *PLAY 4X*   **G**

5 **A**   *Guitar/Harmonica in F*

C   **G**

9   **C**   **G**

B

13   **C**   **G**

17   **C**   1   **G**

26

8. Zz ack-a (CD Track 17)

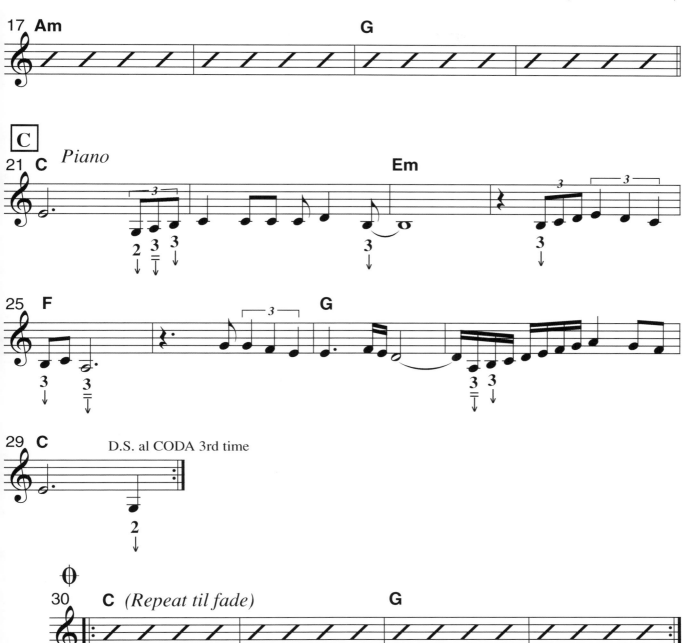

9. Drrrr (CD Track 19)

The chug

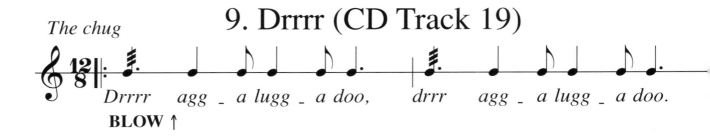

Drrrr agg _ a lugg _ a doo,   drrr   agg _ a lugg _ a doo.

BLOW ↑

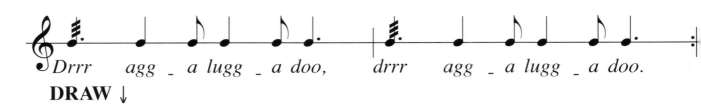

Drrr   agg _ a lugg _ a doo,   drrr   agg _ a lugg _ a doo.

DRAW ↓

The track
Reggae (swing quarter notes) ♩ = 135

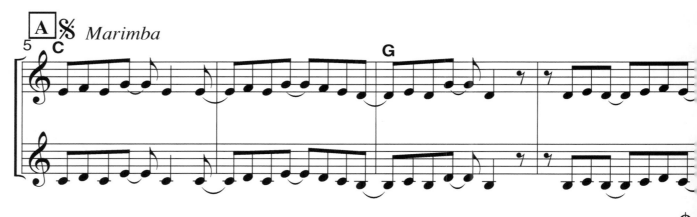

30

9. Drrr (CD Track 19)

31

11. I would like a chicken tikka (CD Track 23)

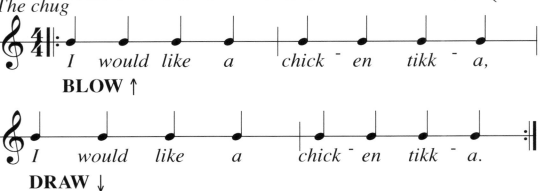

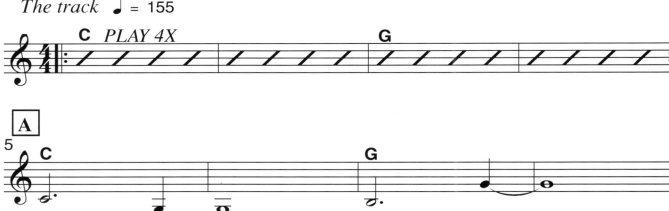

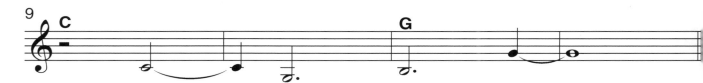

11. I would like a chicken tikka (CD Track 23)

PART 3

TRAINSOUNDS

That's the end of the simple chugging phrases. Each one has merely been a starting point for you to explore. Now you can change the words or even make up your own phrases. Don't forget that if you turn the balance to the left on your CD player you will only hear the backing music. This will give you the space to improvise and try out your own ideas.

There follows a series of phrases that are all train–type sounds. The breathing pattern is more difficult so follow the instructions and listen carefully to the CD. A good project for you would be to learn them all individually and eventually run them all together adding in a few new ones of your own. If you want some inspiration listen to some of the older players like Deford Bailey, Noah Lewis, Jed Davenport and the wondrous Sonny Terry, who has personally influenced me a great deal.

After the trainsounds you will find two extra tracks included here just for fun. 'Dog' is the hardest track on the CD! So, enjoy.

12. Zz acka – Trainsound 1 (CD Track 27)

The chug

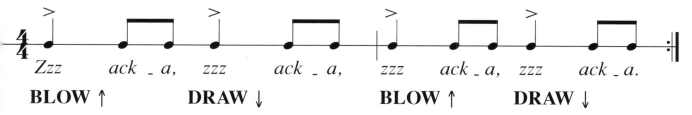

13. Tikka hoo – Trainsound 2 (CD Track 29)

The chug

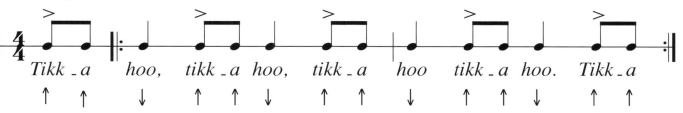

14. Tikka hoo, tikka duddeley –
Trainsound 3 (CD Track 31)

The chug

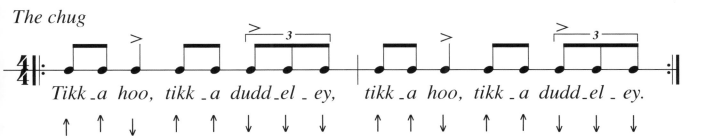

15. Hooka tikka – Trainsound 4 (CD Track 33)

The chug

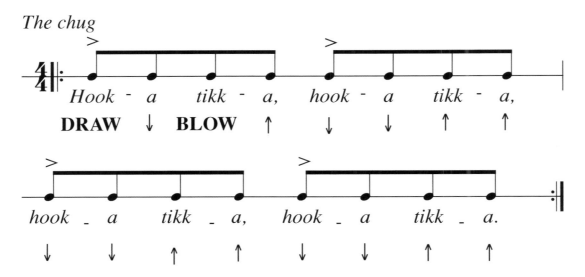

16. Woww – Trainsound 5 (CD Track 35)

The chug

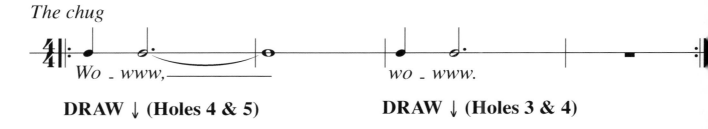

17. Duck (CD Track 37)

The chug

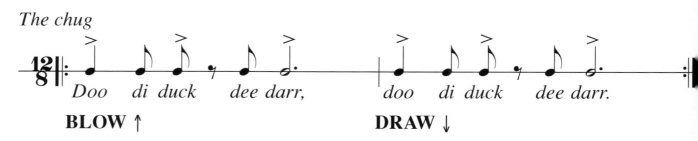

18. Dog (CD Track 39)

The chug

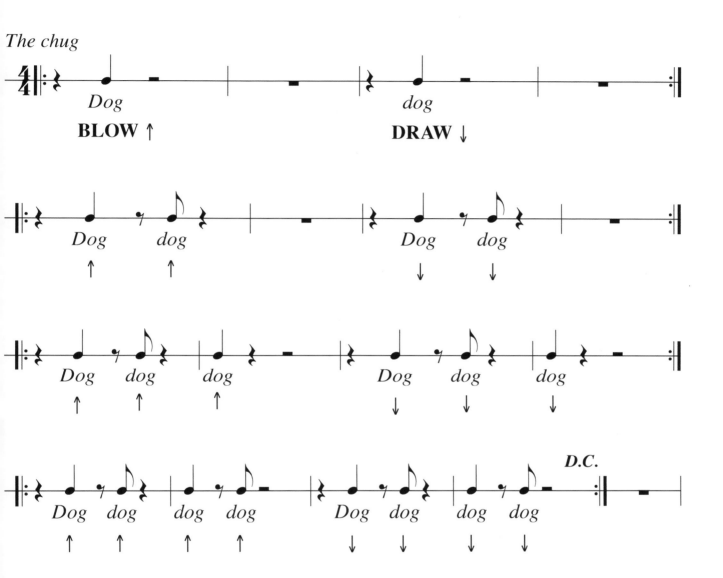

SCUPPERED (CD TRACK 41)

This final 'hidden' track was specially composed to show off a little of the harmonica's potential and also include some of the chugging technique developed over the previous tracks of the CD. It was composed using modern recording techniques and is a combination of live instruments and synthesizers. I wrote the main melody and then had Ben perform this in short sections to a metronome click or a drum track. In addition to this he performed the improvisation sections and then, having recorded them all digitally, I was able to take each piece of harmonica performance and build the backing track around it. Then the whole thing was mixed in the computer." Paul Lennon

"Yes, it was an interesting composing technique – rather like cut and paste in word processing! I used four different harmonicas for this number – a high F# and a low F# in 2nd position, a B in 3rd position and a C# in 1st position. The piece is in C# so each harmonica is also played in the key of C#. It sounds a little confusing but it's true, trust me! Anyway, enjoy the piece." Ben Hewlett

FINAL THOUGHTS

Well done, you've got to the end. Now do it again, and again, and again; wear the CD out. Take the motto 'constant systematic practice' as your guide and you will become an expert player.

Don't forget the many different ways to use this CD/Book package:

1. Chugging – follow the CD instructions.

2. Make up your own 'chugging' phrases (turn balance left).

3. Learn the tunes and play them with the CD. They can also be played an octave higher or lower than written for those wanting a serious challenge.

4. Play the duets with other players.

5. Use harmonicas in different keys to play the tunes or to improvise with. Try F and G as first choices.

6. Improvise with the tracks using simple ideas such as: (i) Play the root notes of the chords i.e. in a bar marked C play a C on the harmonica and if it's Am (A minor) play an A. (ii) Play the first three notes of the scale that starts on each root note i.e. for a C chord play C, D & E. (iii) Play a pentatonic (five note) scale over each chord i.e. for C play C, D, E, G & A (this is called the major pentatonic scale).

As mentioned before you can use the interactive nature of this CD by changing the balance on your CD player so that you are playing on your own with the backing band.

Other CD/book packages are now available in this series:

1. ***The Search for the Single Note*** (The next choice for you.)
2. ***Bones of the Blues*** - 8 easy pentatonic tunes in 4 keys on one harp (the next choice after that).
3. ***Harpscool Mastermix 1*** - chugs, riffs and tunes
4. ***Note - bending*** - the mystery is revealed!
5. ***101 Blues Riffs*** – 20 styles of blues riffs
6. ***The Blues*** – harder tunes in 7 keys on one harp.
7. ***Funky Nursery*** - Easy tunes with cool and funky backing tracks.
8. ***Funky Christmas*** - Easy tunes with cool and funky backing tracks.

Volumes 1, 2, 7, and 8 require NO note bending skills so are fine for new players.

Visit the website – www.harmonicaworld.com to find out more about these products and other harmonica-related materials. You can also email us at ben@harmonicaworld.com.

Biogs: BEN HEWLETT (b. 1959)

Ben Hewlett became a musician at the age of ten in 1969 learning the trumpet. He went through the school system of exams and performances, finally escaping the mandatory classical repertoire with the discovery of Louis Armstrong and Dizzy Gillespie. He was a minor third addict at fourteen and still has a passion for jazz and blues.

Godfather Dennis Corble gave Ben a harmonica at the age of 7 thus unknowingly sowing the seeds of a lifelong love of this instrument!

At twenty-eight a decade of 'not much music' was ended when, after endless screenings of the Blues Brothers film, Ben bought his first harmonica (in the key of E following the music stores' advice as the best key for Blues) and he resumed work on minor thirds as well as doing extensive research into the origins of the songs recorded by the Blues Brothers Band. He found that he could easily do on the harmonica all the things he had been unsuccessfully trying to do on the trumpet.

He came across some solo Sonny Terry recordings, was listening to lots of recorded blues, and going to see blues bands. One of the first was Paul Lamb's band, which had a Tuesday night residency at a London Pub near where Ben lived, and after a while he asked Paul Lamb for a lesson or two. Paul's main advice was to study Sonny Terry to get the rhythm, chugging and tone sorted out –years later he still studies Sonny Terry.

The next significant player Ben met was Brendan Power. This happened through the UK's National Harmonica League and resulted in him having lessons with Brendan. Ben was now in a blues band (within a year of starting harmonica) doing pub gigs around London, and did so for the next ten years until he left London for the West Country – home. Brendan asked Ben to babysit his harmonica evening class for a night and then for a term and then on a permanent basis, so soon he was teaching five classes a week and had to go to college to learn how to teach music in group workshops.

Two years later he was a qualified Music Workshop Leader and working full time teaching music in different settings – such as with disabled people using music technology; working at day centres for adults with learning difficulties; the harmonica workshops; harmonica lessons in schools; and giving private lessons at home. He met Paul Lennon at one of the colleges where Paul was teaching 'ear training' and 'jazz harmony'.

Since leaving London Ben has gone into full time harmonica teaching. In 2002 he successfully completed the teaching qualification 'Certificate of Teaching, Associated Board of the Royal Schools of Music' (CTABRSM).

In 2006 he had thirty two schools a week to visit with five hundred students – becoming by default the only full-time professional harmonica teacher in the UK. His teaching business (HarpsCool) had (in 2006) nine harmonica teachers to spread the harmonica word. He has also run a Blues Band workshop for ten years to provide a setting for new harp players to gain band experience, also harmonica night school classes, Saturday 'learn to play in a day' courses all over the west of England, and continues to teach many private students.

Fun creations 2000-2003:

- Guinness World record for 'Largest Harmonica Ensemble'.
- 100 Children dressed as the Blues Brothers playing the Peter Gunn Theme on harmonicas to an audience of 2,500.
- Introduced a school full of 350 children to 'chugging' in one day and had them perform to parents and staff.

- His students have received countless UK Harmonica Championship titles! Recent study and Harmonica high spots:
- A week of Jazz on the diatonic at the Jamey Aebersold summer school in London
- A week of study in Germany (in Trossingen – home of the Hohner Harmonica) learning with Joe Filisko, Steve Baker, Rick Epping, and Carlos Del Junco.
- A week of study in the US at the SPAH.org annual conference where he received an invitation to teach. He studied with Richard Sleigh (whose custom marine bands are Ben's main choice of instrument) Joe Filisko, Jimmy Conway, David Barrett, Phil Duncan, Alan Radcliffe Holmes and lots more experts.
- A week studying with the extraordinary Howard Levy – best player on this planet.
- A trip to Thailand to research the origin of the Harmonica – the Khaen. He filmed the making of these instruments and even studied traditional playing in Lao with Achan Kamsuan, the 'by appointment' Khaen instructor to the Thai Royal family!
- Two talks on diatonic harmonica - one to students at a Singapore University and the other to HAS – Harmonica Aficionados Singapore.

The whole 'CHUGGING' idea was born and developed as the very best way to get people started on harmonica. Ben based it on Sonny Terry's way of playing rhythms and his articulations.

It resulted from years of experimentation with different methods of introducing people to playing – many thousands of people in fact. It has proven to be extremely popular and a very successful foundation for playing harmonica as it builds rhythm and breathing skills quickly and painlessly. Only one person didn't like it and that was Larry Adler – read his quote on page 49.

After the idea of creating a backing track for people to play along with, Ben got together with Paul Lennon and came up with the ideas that have led to a fruitful and exciting partnership.

Paul has amazing musical skills – he is able to play guitar, violin, bass, piano, keyboards and therefore anything through keyboards on the computer - all up to session and concert standard. He has been a professional teacher of all those instruments and more for over twenty years in the world of classical, jazz, blues, and most other styles of music. He is also a composer who owns a very well-equipped recording studio in Kent, UK.

With Paul's talents and Ben's drive and passion for teaching the harmonica, they have broken new ground and come up with an excellent method for learning the diatonic harmonica in a progressive way.

In 2003 Bristol University asked Ben to put on a 'corporate' team building session in a staff development week.

From this was born 'Blues Jam Factory'. It is now a successful corporate team-building and training operation with a growing client base including DHL/Exel, Lloyds TSB, Sanofi Aventis, TBL, The Hemsley Fraser Group, Instant Teamwork, Spice UK and many more in the pipeline including Shell, KPMG and Centrex. This typically one-hour event is available in all English speaking countries including North America. Contact Ben for a promotional DVD to see how much this amazing program can energize YOUR company/group/social set.

PAUL LENNON L.T.C.L. (b. 1957)

Paul is a composer/arranger and multi-instrumentalist and teacher. A former pupil of Bishop Wordsworth School, Salisbury and former member and leader of the Wiltshire Youth and Salisbury Junior Orchestras on violin. He also played in rock and folk bands in the Salisbury area from the age of 15 onwards and later graduate from Trinity College of Music, London in violin, piano and composition (1978-80). Paul has been involved in many classical/light music ventures including orchestras, a flute quartet, a duo with cello and even a 1930's cabaret act. He went on to play bass, guitar, violin and keyboards in various bands. From 1988–91 he was the bass player and a composer/arranger with EPJ, a 13-piece modern jazz big band. He played guitar, keyboards and vocals in a 4-piece pop band, then violin in a duo with guitar until mid 1996, followed by piano in his own original jazz quartet with guitar, bass and drums.

In 1998, a collaboration with The Booming Cherries, a contemporary dance troupe, he produced Gravy Bones, a jazz oriented dance work. The following year he wrote and recorded the score for an adaptation of King Arthur, a current production by the Spiral Arts dance-theatre company. Other works include string quartets, pieces for flute and piano/guitar and solo piano. All these works reflect an eclectic experience and a leaning towards music for dramatic and visual media. He writes from his Kent-based home recording studio and has composed and produced many albums there including playalongs for harmonica with Ben Hewlett and spoken-word material with Shaun de Warren and Marietta Pinto-Hayes.

He has produced books on Music Training Basics, Practicing and Ear-Training as well as collections of pieces for piano, violin, guitar and flute. From 1993 Paul taught at the City Literary Institute in London and wrote a three-year jazz harmony and ear-training course.

From July 2001 to June 2002 Paul played bass and shared lead vocals in a band based in Claridges Hotel in London during which time he built a large pad of vocal material. From then he played in various duos on violin with Charles Alexander, Jamey Moore and Dominic Grant (guitar) and on piano and guitar with saxophonist Howard Turner. Since the summer 2002 he has studied violin and piano on the Jamey Aebersold Jazz Summer Schools in London for three years running. As a music editor and copyist he has worked for many years with Dave Hewson on his projects for KPM/EMI with at least eight albums to Paul's credit. 2002 also saw the recording of a harmonica sample album with Ben Hewlett for ZERO-G, a major sample company.

Currently Paul is very involved in composition and recording particularly with Ben Hewlett on the ongoing Harmonica Course and also his own playalong projects for guitar and piano. Another major project is writing and recording of material for a website that will cater for dance schools, competitions and festivals by producing CDs and tracks for download.

Paul can be contacted at: paul@paullennon.com

Harmonica tablature (tab) chart

Diatonic notes where ↑ = BLOW and ↓ = DRAW

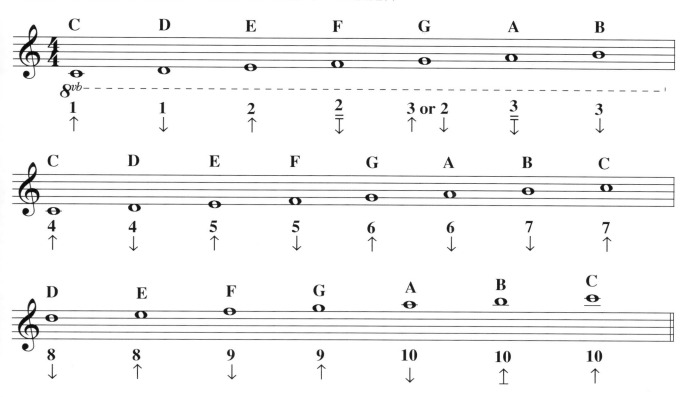

Chromatic notes – all these notes need to be bent (see below)

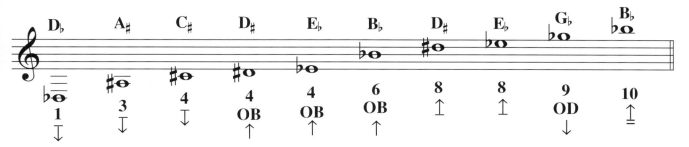

half-step	**half-step**
$\overline{\underset{\downarrow}{}}$ = one semitone drawbend	$\overline{\underset{\uparrow}{}}$ = one semitone blowbend
whole-step	**whole-step**
$\underset{\downarrow}{=}$ = two semitone drawbend	$\underset{\uparrow}{=}$ = two semitone blowbend

OB = overblow (a type of bending)

OD = overdraw (another type of bending)

For more information on bending notes see the Ben Hewlett Harmonica Course volume:
'Note bending – the mystery finally revealed!'

Quotes and reviews

"A great teaching CD – a must for beginners and advanced players as well" – Paul Lamb, winner best UK Blues Harmonica player 1990, 1991, 1992, 1993, 1994 (now in The British Blues Connection Hall of Fame).

"If you want to play like Paul Lamb learn with Ben Hewlett." – PAUL JONES, The Blues Band, BBC RADIO 2, JAZZ FM etc.

"I like it very much and I'm sure a lot of people will benefit from it" – Johnny Mars, 21st Century Blues Prophet.

"This course is just what we need" – M. HOHNER

"A real nice approach, and a wonderful teaching tool for everyone from beginners to intermediates" – Lee Oskar, President, LEE OSKAR HARMONICAS

"A progressive approach" – Anthony Denton, Director of Resources, Leeds College of Music, and expert jazz baritone sax player.

Quotes and reviews

"Simplicity itself" – WB (a blind harmonica student).

"It will appeal to every person who buys a new harmonica" – M. HOHNER (manufacturers of 30 million harmonicas every year since 1930).

"I am playing the Harmonica for 12 years and now I am learning to play the Blues Harp with your courses!!!" – Lisa Fellinger-Laakirchen, Austria.

Ben and Paul have given the world a pretty revolutionary new way of learning the harmonica - not even a trace of "When the Saints"! Concentrating on the blow and draw-chords, Ben quickly gets you playing along to a series of very nicely produced and played instrumentals in a variety of styles. The emphasis is on playing rhythmically, and on the wide range of sounds and effects you can achieve by articulating different sounds into your harp. These range from the relatively sedate "choo choo chooo" to the sublimely bonkers "I would like a chicken tikka" !
MINSTRELS MUSIC – HARMONICAS DIRECT.

"Charlie (6) took to it like a duck to water – quite remarkable how you could get instant music out of it. You avoid all that incredibly boring banging away on one guitar string bit and get straight to the music – incredibly clever." – Chris Logan Turner.

"Very good indeed – pick it up, put in the CD and start playing. Good fun and accessible with dialogue." – M.A. (A visually impaired sax player).

Quotes and reviews

"Thanks again for a great first lesson!! Been chugging ever since but still can't say "took chicka tack chicka took chicka tack diddeley" anywhere near fast enough !!" – Martin Mason.

"The good thing about this CD is that you're instantly making music." – Keith Warmington, BBC RADIO BRISTOL.

"I have listened to the CD (CHUGGING) and feel that it represents good value and if your child follows the instructions and plays along with the music as asked, his/her practice will become more focused and will mean faster progress"– EJ Gibbs, Head of Music, High Littleton School.

"Just picked up a copy of your CD. I am a beginner, having been playing for about a year or so in earnest. It was a good time to be reminded of what I didn't know!! Although there is no substitute for face to face teaching, this is a great way of installing basics. Looking forward to the next installment" – Keith Floodgate, student.

"My congratulation on a job well done." – Pat Missin, HARMONICA Guru

"This is the ultimate format for teaching yourself how to play the harmonica" – Steve Proctor, GAD Former UK Distributor of HERING HARMONICAS (another huge manufacturer).

Quotes and reviews

"This CD is a treasure with simple clear instructions, recorded in top quality sound. A MUST for all to try, not just beginners and Ben makes if FUN! Endorsed by the International Harmonica Organization." – John Walton, PRESIDENT OF THE INTERNATIONAL HARMONICA ORGANIZATION.

"I am not interested in an instrument with missing notes. Therefore while I respect your hard work and educational aims, I cannot give you an appreciative quotation." – LARRY ADLER.

"A great foursome – student, CD, book, and teacher." – Colin Mort, CHAIRMAN OF NATIONAL HARMONICA LEAGUE AND EDITOR OF 'HARMONICA WORLD.'

"Hey, track 41's dead cool.… One day yeah! Have you released the follow up to chugging yet?" – Keven Garner, student.

"Excellent teaching and marvellous materials" – David Adams, ORCHESTRA MANAGER MCO LTD. English Baroque Soloist & Orchestre Revolutionaire et Romantique.

"The evaluations from last year [the summer school] confirmed how popular the Harmonica Lessons were. We would very much like to build on this and concentrate the music lessons solely on one instrument, preferably the Harmonica." – S. Herbert, BRISTOL ROYAL SOCIETY FOR THE BLIND.

Quotes and reviews

"Ben is one of the West's finest Harmonica Players" – Chris Serle, BBC RADIO BRISTOL.

"A fantastic teacher" – VIVA RADIO, LONDON.

"...Harmonica guru, Ben Hewlett." – SOMERSET GUARDIAN.

"Ben is an inspiration to us all" – Edward Enfield (Harry's Dad!) on RADIO 4 'FREE SPIRITS.'

"Ben Hewlett, the respected British harmonica teacher."
– Pat Missin, in HARMONICA WORLD.

"Teaching is Ben's 'raison d'etre', it's what he does and he does it well."
– M. HOHNER.

Quotes and reviews

"A well–thought–out, musical, well–structured and useful resource for harmonica teaching. Great fun to use." – Paul Matthews, Head of BRISTOL COUNTY COUNCIL SCHOOLS MUSIC SERVICES.

"Ben, I've received Chugging, been trying it out and I'm impressed. The book is easy to follow and the CD is great. In particular, I like the play–along tracks being about 2 and 1/4 minutes long. Being able to practice the phrases and play rhythmically and continuously for about a song length period of time makes a refreshing change from playing along to the short bursts recorded on the CDs of other music books. I feel like I am beginning to make some music at last! I look forward to learning this volume and buying the next. I didn't know rythmn harmonica could be so much fun.
Thanks Ben and Paul, Cheers, Ty"

"Hello Ben, Thanks for the chuggers course book and CD. As I said, I am not used to playing on a Richter tuned harp. So I got my chord harmonica and joined in, It's fantastic. This could well be turned into a chord harmonica course. There are no such books on the market these days. Al Smith wrote one in the 70s but was done by hand and not looking professional. I am sure that, including me, there will be players also looking for volume II. A job well done. Very best wishes, Art Daane" (One of the grandees of the harmonica!)

"As a person who has grown blasé about tutor books especially those for beginners, and fed up with inane approaches and sameness, I was astonished to find myself wanting to get on to the next page because the ideas sucked me in. I had to reach for my harmonica and try what was being taught! I really do think that Ben and Paul have a winner here. I am very pleased to see that the harmonica tablature which assists players in the very early stages is quickly abandoned as you get to know where the notes are. Within the first couple of pages tab is only used to introduced new notes of effects." Douglas Tate, President of SPAH.org - The biggest harmonica community in the U.S.A.

Printed in Great Britain
by Amazon